IMAGES
of America

CHICAGO'S
SOUTH SHORE

The author's father, Hugo (Hugh) W. Celander Jr., and grandfather, Hugo W. Celander Sr., stroll through South Shore in November 1924. Hugh Celander Jr. became a local photographer whose own photographs, along with other collected images, are featured in this book. Hugo Celander Sr. was in real estate. This book, which chronicles the development of Chicago's South Shore area through the use of historic photographs, is dedicated to them.

IMAGES
of America

CHICAGO'S
SOUTH SHORE

Charles Celander

ARCADIA
PUBLISHING

Published by Arcadia Publishing
Charleston, South Carolina

Library of Congress Catalog Card Number: 2001092767

For all general information contact Arcadia Publishing at:
Telephone 843-853-2070
Fax 843-853-0044
E-mail sales@arcadiapublishing.com
For customer service and orders:
Toll-Free 1-888-313-2665

Visit us on the Internet at www.arcadiapublishing.com

A typical South Shore street, Oglesby Avenue runs the length of the neighborhood.

CONTENTS

Celander Studio opened as a neighborhood studio in 1951. Although legal photography was the original focus of the business, weddings, portraits, and local commercial work soon dominated. What began as photographic evidence for courtroom use ultimately became documentation of the neighborhood.

INTRODUCTION

This book is not intended to be the final word on the history of Chicago's South Shore community. It is instead an opportunity to review its story from a very specific point of view—that of a neighborhood photographer in the 1950s and 1960s.

My father, Hugh Celander, a native of South Shore, and my mother, Marian Celander, owned and operated a photography studio on 79th Street from the early 1950s to the early 1970s. They documented many of the personal and public events of South Shore during that time, as well as the cityscape itself. Their work brought them into the lives of others, as they photographed weddings, children, and anniversaries. It took them into adjacent neighborhoods where, together with friends and colleagues, they pursued their love of photography throughout the city. In addition, customers whose families had originally settled or helped develop the neighborhood would occasionally bring in old photographs to be restored. As a result, my father amassed an eclectic collection of images, including views of South Shore, pictures from the land developments of the 1920s, and photographs of the post-war development in the 1950s and 1960s.

After closing his studio around 1970, my father discarded many thousands of negatives, choosing to keep only those of personal or historical interest. Many are gathered here. Gone are the portraits and wedding pictures of others. Gone also are many of the historical subjects he recorded. Sadly, gone too are many of my father's own memories. Senility has stolen much of his past, and his photographs are now very nearly his only memories.

Today it is hard to imagine the South Shore neighborhood as anything but a part of Chicago. The community's mature, urban nature disguises its evolution from marshland to farmland, and from suburb to city neighborhood. Located between Jackson Park and 79th Street, and from Lake Michigan to Stony Island, the marshland of the 1800s was first settled by German and Scandinavian truck and flower farmers. The few roads through the area were dotted with an occasional roadhouse, servicing travelers on their way to Chicago, but not much else. Few saw the potential of the swampy land south of the city limits at 35th Street, but events would conspire to create great opportunity for those who did. Investors in the area included Chicago Mayor (Long) John Wentworth, Senator Stephen A. Douglas, and a young attorney and entrepreneur by the name of Paul Cornell.

During the mid-1850s, Cornell negotiated a deal with the Illinois Central Railroad, which, at that time, needed a right of way through land that he owned. He offered to sell a portion of this land to the railroad in return for a commitment that they provide passenger service between Chicago and a town that he was to build—Hyde Park. Although not an immediate success, over the years the service was gradually extended to Parkside, another Cornell development, located at 70th Street. Then, in 1871, the Great Chicago Fire drove many families out of the city in search of housing that was safe, and preferably fireproof. As demand for housing outside the city increased, so did the demand for transportation. The Illinois Central responded, and momentum to develop the area that would be South Shore began.

South of the marshes, along the Calumet River, the area was seeing tremendous industrial development. Access to the Great Lakes, the inland waterways, and to railroads would bring the steel industry to an area called Irondale and to its neighbor, South Chicago. The Illinois Central decided to run a passenger line through South Shore to South Chicago in 1881. The Bryn Mawr, Windsor Park, and Cheltenham depots serviced this small but exploding population. By 1889, communities like Essex and Parkside merged with South Shore, and the entire area including Hyde Park became part of the city of Chicago, just in time to start planning for a World's Fair.

For some, the opening of the World's Columbian Exposition of 1893 in Jackson Park was an opportunity to discover a new land. The traffic to the south side of Chicago for the Fair was enormous, and the Illinois Central Railway was there to serve as the common man's *Nina*, *Pinta*, and *Santa Maria*. The transportation infrastructure built up steam, and the momentum continued to expand southern development.

In 1906, the South Shore Country Club was formed with an exclusively white, Protestant membership. Over the years, other groups would follow suit and pursue a middle-class lifestyle in the developing community. A huge wave of construction began after the First World War, and the 1920s would witness the largest development period in South Shore's history. Individual bricklayers would be stacking eight hundred to one thousand bricks per day in an attempt to keep up with the demands of developers and contractors. This dynamic period was brought to a swift halt by the stock market crash and resulting depression.

The end of World War II brought with it a new boom in housing demand and the shifts in population that went along with it. As quality housing became harder to find in Chicago, black families began moving into South Shore. Issues of integration, racial steering, and stabilization of neighborhoods rose above South Shore's horizon and reached a zenith in the 1960s and 1970s. The politics of race became an overwhelming issue for a majority of the white ethnic populations of South Shore, and most fled in the end.

The South Shore Country Club was purchased by the Chicago Park District in 1974 and is now a public facility.

One

THE SETTLERS AND DEVELOPMENTS SOUTH OF CHICAGO

On July 21, 1856, a special Illinois Central suburban train made a round-trip to what is now 53rd Street. It was a pivotal point in the plans of a young Chicago lawyer by the name of Paul Cornell, and a pivotal point in the development of what would later become South Shore. Cornell owned a 300-acre tract of undeveloped land that he planned to subdivide. A proposal to sell 60 acres to the railroad, on the condition that a "Hyde Park" station offering daily passenger service to Chicago be built on the property was accepted. The train pictured here ran the route in 1884.

In the late 1800s, the land south of Jackson Park contained great sand dunes along the lake, gradually giving way to bogs and sloughs inland. In 1900, hunting at 79th Street and Euclid Avenue was still popular.

Where patches of land rose above the water level, small flower and "truck" farms were built. An 1895 view, looking north from 79th Street and Chappel Avenue, shows the Krause family farm and greenhouse, located at 78th Street and Jeffery Boulevard.

In 1898, the Krause family farm was representative of the first settlers to the area—Scandinavian and European truck farmers and greenhousemen who first migrated to the area in the 1850s.

This is another view of the Krause farm, taken in 1895, looking north on Jeffery Boulevard from a point just north of 79th Street.

The Clemenson family had already been farming in the area for 16 years when this photograph was taken in 1908. Christian Clemenson came to America from Denmark in 1892 to work on the Columbian Exposition of 1893. He rented 20 acres at 81st Street and Burnham Avenue where he created a family flower farm.

The Clemenson family maintained a retail flower shop at 7801 South Exchange Avenue, which existed in the same location until 1978, when it relocated to south suburban Glenwood. Currently, Clemenson's Florist continues to operate in Flossmoor.

In 1882, the Illinois Central Railroad began construction of a 4.7-mile branch that extended east from the main line at 69th Street to Exchange Avenue (then named Railroad Avenue) and south to the steel mills of South Chicago. The South Chicago station opened on September 2, 1883, and is seen here in 1910. The wooden passenger cars also began serving the Bryn Mawr, Windsor Park, and Cheltenham stations, which were built about the same time as the South Chicago station.

In 1889, the same year that Hyde Park Township was annexed to Chicago, a developer named Frank Bennett built one hundred frame houses on 5 acres of land between 71st and 72nd Streets on Euclid Avenue. This formed the development known as Parkside. Parkside was soon joined by the Essex development to the south. This 1896 photograph shows the Bryn Mawr Illinois Central station on 71st Street, around which the community had been developing.

In 1915, this view of the Bryn Mawr station shows development as it existed looking east along an unpaved 71st Street.

Another view of the Bryn Mawr Illinois Central Railroad station is pictured here, looking west down 71st Street sometime prior to 1920.

The Windsor Park station, at 75th Street and Exchange Avenue, was established when service to South Chicago began in 1883. It is shown here in an 1896 photograph.

Another view of the Windsor Park station is shown here in a photograph taken after 1900.

The Brown Coal Company office, built in 1887, was located at 75th Street and Exchange Avenue, and is pictured here in 1898.

This is a view looking west on 79th Street near Exchange after 1900.

Seen here, in the first of two views of the Cheltenham station, is a coal car that supplied steam engines on the South Chicago leg of the Illinois Central suburban line. The center platform is also visible in this c. 1900 photograph. The two-story station provided living quarters upstairs for the switchman.

In this earlier 1895 view, the switchman's tower, which survived long past the station itself, can be seen. The Cheltenham was built at the same time as the Jeffery and Windsor Park stations and was intended to serve the isolated homes between the main line and the steel mill settlements.

In 1959, all that remained of the original 1880s station was the switchman's tower. The building in the background to the right of the flagman's house is also visible in photographs of the original station.

The old Cheltenham station, along with the other stations of the era, was demolished when the line was electrified in 1926. The frame station pictured above replaced the individual styles of the originals and provided a uniform look. The photograph shown here was taken in 1959.

The station at 83rd Street and Exchange Avenue is pictured here in 1896.

In 1902, the area surrounding 75th Street and Lake Michigan was filled with boardwalks, bathing piers, bathhouses, dance halls, and refreshment stands. The Manhattan Beach Pavilion,

A view of the same area in 1959 is pictured above. Rainbow Beach extends south in the background.

built by Phillip Cleys, was destroyed by fire in 1922.

In 1908, the pavilions at Manhattan and Windsor Beaches offered an array of amusements.

Farther south, at 87th Street, an amusement park called "The Last Days of Pompeii" featured hot air balloon rides landing at the Clemenson farm, where rides back were available for a quarter.

In this 1913 photograph, a lone Chicago bungalow faces the tracks along the rutted dirt intersection of 72nd Street and Exchange Avenue.

Streetcars brought amusement seekers to and from the lakefront pavilions at 75th Street. A portion of the streetcar turnaround is visible in this picture.

Fassbinder's Barber Shop, on the north side of 75th Street near Exchange Avenue, is seen in this photograph from the early 1900s. The original photograph identifies the two gentlemen on the left as the Moe brothers—Gisle Moe at left and Reider Moe at right. The connection is undocumented.

This is the Windsor Park station in a view taken around 1905.

"Jonas Hall," located on the northeast corner of 75th Street and Coles Avenue, is pictured here in an undated photograph. Gent and Clem Funeral Home was located on the first floor of the building.

Looking east on 79th Street towards Exchange Avenue, this undated photograph shows the streetcar tracks and a horse and wagon in the distance. Progress in early South Shore saw plank walkways and muddy streets replaced with sidewalks (seen here) and sewers.

Two

1893

THE WORLD DISCOVERS
THE SOUTH SIDE

The term "Windy City" became associated with Chicago not as a description of climate, but of self-promotion. Supporters of Chicago as the site of the 1893 World's Fair delivered enough "hot air" to win the day. With Chicago selected, Jackson Park, a locale just north of South Shore and adjacent to Hyde Park, was chosen for the site of the event. John Root and Daniel Burnham led the building architects, and Frederick Law Olmsted designed the landscaping for the Fair.

Looking south in this 1954 aerial view over Jackson Park, some landmarks from the 1893 Columbian Exposition are still visible. The lagoons and The Wooded Island are located right and center, and the Manufacturers Building would have been located in the open area between the Lake and the Lagoon. After the fair, Frederick Law Olmsted's vision for the fairgrounds was revised, as Jackson Park received a final redesign.

Illinois Central Railroad's support of the Jackson Park location for the Columbian Exposition promoted the best interests of both the railroad and the south side. The boom of economic activity associated with the fair, along with demands for safer housing after the Great Chicago Fire of 1871, increased pressure to develop areas immediately south of the city limits. Construction of the fair can be seen in this 1892 photograph looking east on 65th Street.

Seen here at the Van Buren Street station in 1893, special passenger cars called "Sullivans," named after an Illinois Central Railroad executive, were built to service the World's Fair. Twelve doors down, each side loaded and unloaded passengers swiftly from the bench seats placed down the center of each car. Sullivans were designed to be converted into freight cars after the fair.

The Palace of Fine Arts at the 1893 World's Fair was designed by Charles B. Atwood. Concerned for the safety of the artworks installed within, it was one of the few buildings constructed of brick, and thus fireproof. The majority of the fair's buildings were constructed with staff—a mixture of plaster, cement, and jute fiber. Most of those buildings were destroyed by fire in the years immediately following the event. The Palace of Fine Arts would later become the Museum of Science and Industry, pictured here in 1938.

This replica of Columbus's flagship was constructed for the World's Fair. Anchored in the lagoons of Jackson Park for several decades after the fair, it was eventually destroyed by fire sometime after this photograph was taken in 1938.

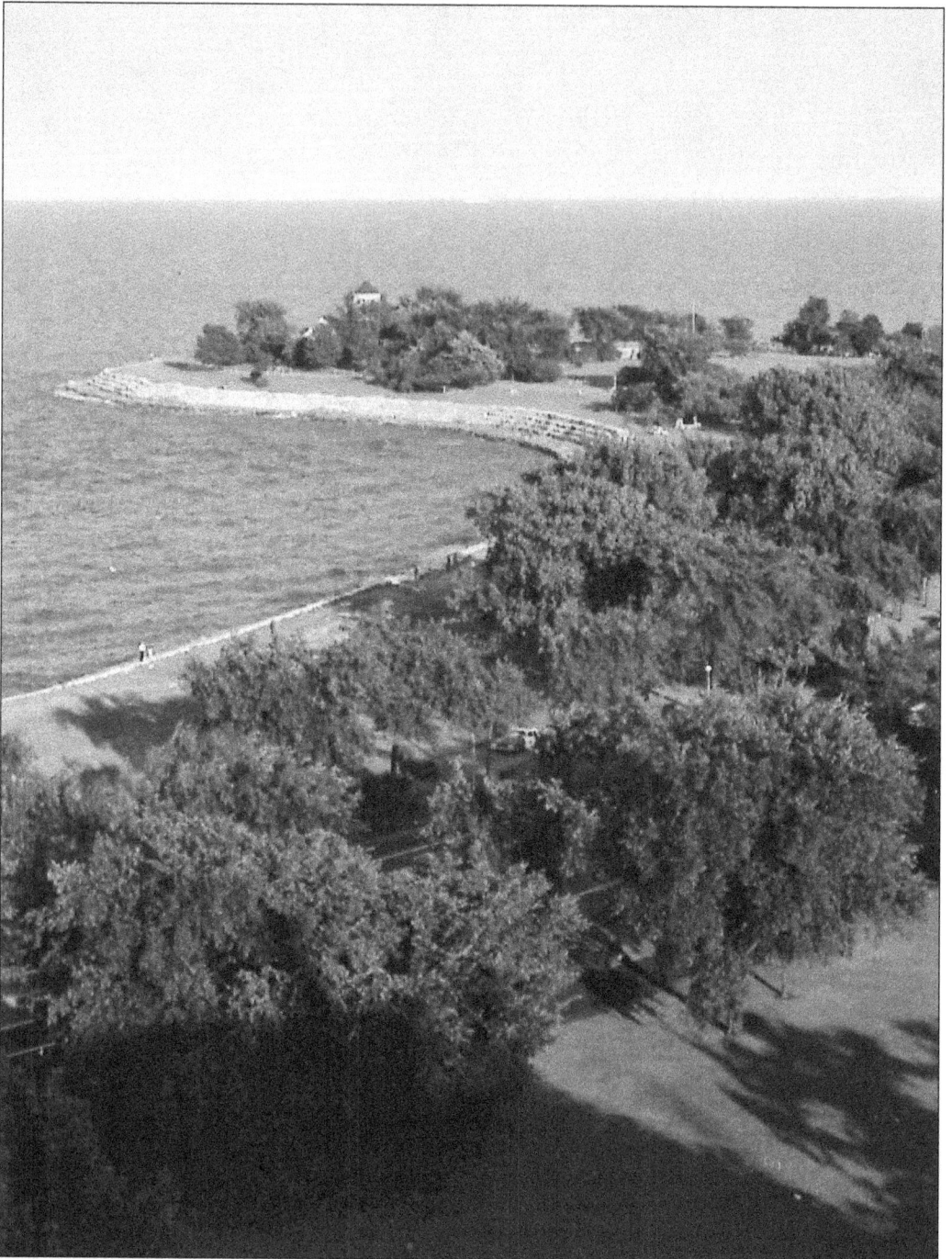

Adjacent to Jackson Park, Promotory Point at 55th Street and the lake is the southernmost point of Burnham Park and was designed by landscape architect Alfred Caldwell. During the construction of the 1893 World's Fair, nearby homes displaced by the canals were floated south to what is now Rainbow Beach. Some of these structures can still be seen directly adjacent to the beach. The lots have two houses, one directly behind the other, along the east side of South Shore Drive.

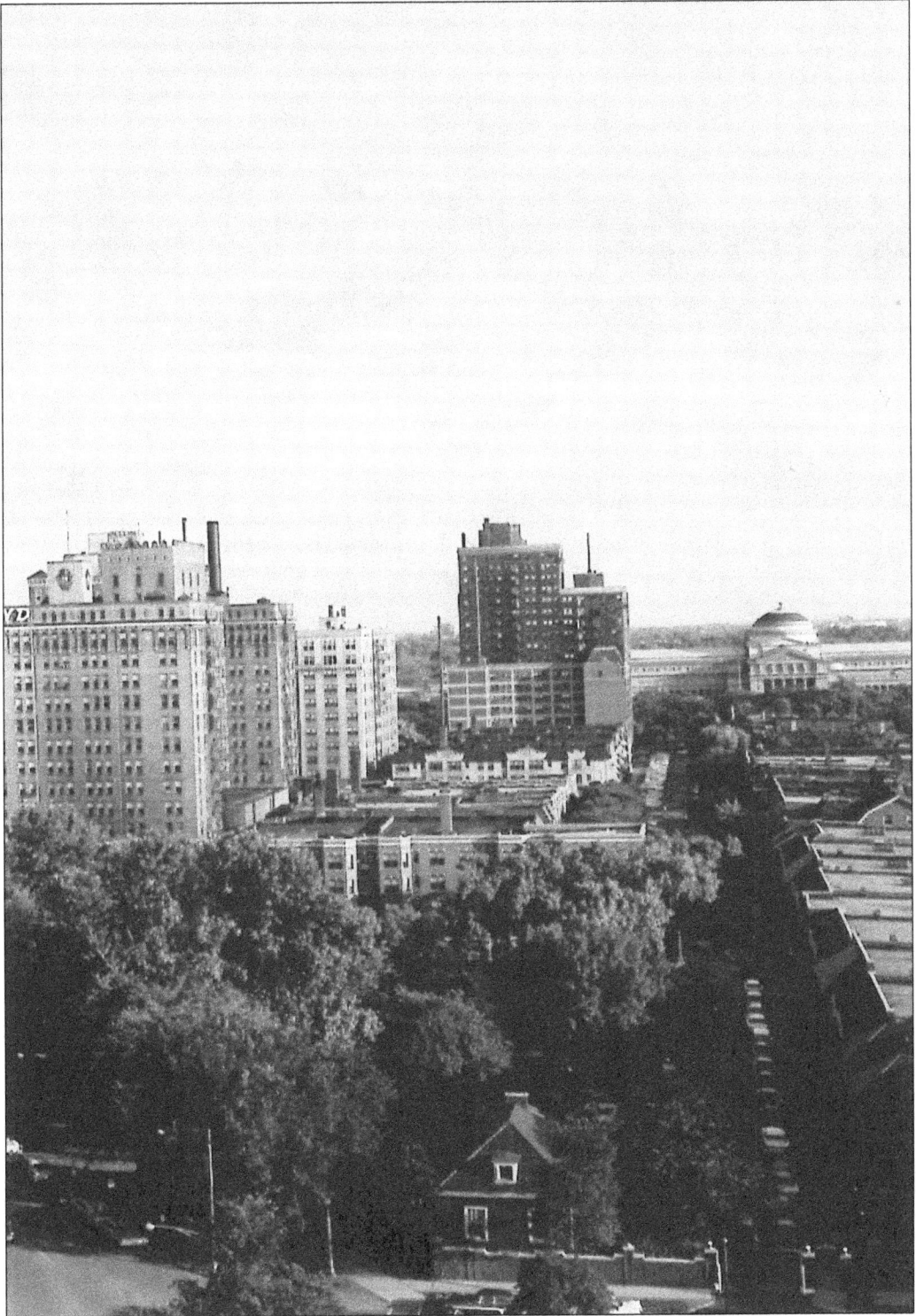

This view from atop the Sherry Hotel in 1960 looks south toward the Shoreland Hotel and the Museum of Science and Industry.

Jackson Park, designed by Frederick Law Olmsted, was carved from sloughs in time for the 1893 World's Fair. The Jackson Park Coast Guard station, built in 1906, is seen here in 1938.

The Coast Guard station is seen here in an opposite view, across the inlet. This complex of lagoons, marinas, and inlets grew out of the system used to flood the canals and basins of the Columbian Exposition and were reworked in an 1895 park plan.

The effect of the World's Fair of 1893 was most directly felt by Hyde Park, which witnessed a boom in new hotels to accommodate visitors. Although South Shore benefited to a degree—Paul Cornell built the Calumet Hotel at 75th Street and Exchange Avenue—much of the new construction associated with the fair was needed to house workers who were responsible for building and running the event. Such was the case with this building at 74th Street and Phillips Avenue, seen here in 1962. Other, more temporary quarters for workers sprang up along South Shore Drive and have long since vanished.

Delaware House, the structure representing the state of Delaware at the 1893 Columbian Exposition, was floated on Lake Michigan and down the Wolf River which, at the time, connected Lake Michigan with Wolf Lake. It was resettled there along the southwest shore of the smaller lake, until demolished sometime after this photograph was taken in 1957. The house was constructed entirely of native Delaware lumber and cost $7,500 to build at the time of the Fair.

A one-third-size reproduction of "The Republic," the statue by Daniel Chester French displayed at the Exposition, now stands in Jackson Park near the site of the original.

Three

COUNTRY CLUB YEARS AND DEVELOPMENT OF SOUTH SHORE

By the 1880s, the Washington Park area west of Hyde Park had become an exclusively middle-class, Protestant neighborhood. After the 1893 World's Fair, housing and transportation in the area became more available, and the neighborhood began to change when working-class Irish Catholic families arrived. By 1905 the Washington Park Club closed, as many of its former members moved to South Shore. In 1906 the South Shore County Club was chartered, providing an exclusive social institution for those attracted to the developing neighborhood.

Ironically, Irish Catholics would soon find their way to South Shore, as Jews moved into Washington Park. The Jewish families followed the Catholics, and a pattern was established. Over the years, different ethnic and racial groups migrated through the south side into South Shore.

The original clubhouse, built when the club was chartered in 1906, was replaced in 1916 with the Mediterranean-style structure most commonly identified with the South Shore Country Club. Shown here in 1954, the country club was purchased by the Chicago Park District in 1973. Now public, it hosts jazz concerts, among other events, and continues a fine golf tradition.

Shown above is an aerial view of South Shore Country Club and the South Shore skyline in 1954.

The area between 67th and 69th Streets from Jeffery Boulevard to Creiger Avenue stood vacant until 1905, when Frank Bennett, the developer of nearby Parkside, began a development on the ridge overlooking Jackson Park. An area of upper-class homes, it became known as the Jackson Park Highlands. This example of the Classical Revival style was built in 1905 near 68th Street and Euclid Avenue.

Built in 1915 near 68th Street and Euclid Avenue, this example of American 4-Square style was planned by John R. Stone, an architect known for traditional apartment building and row house designs.

This residence near 68th Street and Constance Avenue was built during the later development of the Highlands, around 1920.

Designed by Charles Faulkner and built in 1920, this residence on Constance Avenue is an example of Colonial Revival architecture. Like many of the homes in the Jackson Park Highlands, it is listed in the Chicago Historic Resources Survey.

William Pruyn Jr. designed this Tudor Revival at 7200 Crandon Avenue in 1917. Pruyn was the son of a contractor who worked for Hoaratio Wilson, a popular architect responsible for many Hyde Park homes between 1897 and 1910.

This view looks west on 79th Street at Exchange in a photograph taken after 1900. The original Ringer Real Estate office can be seen across the intersection on the right.

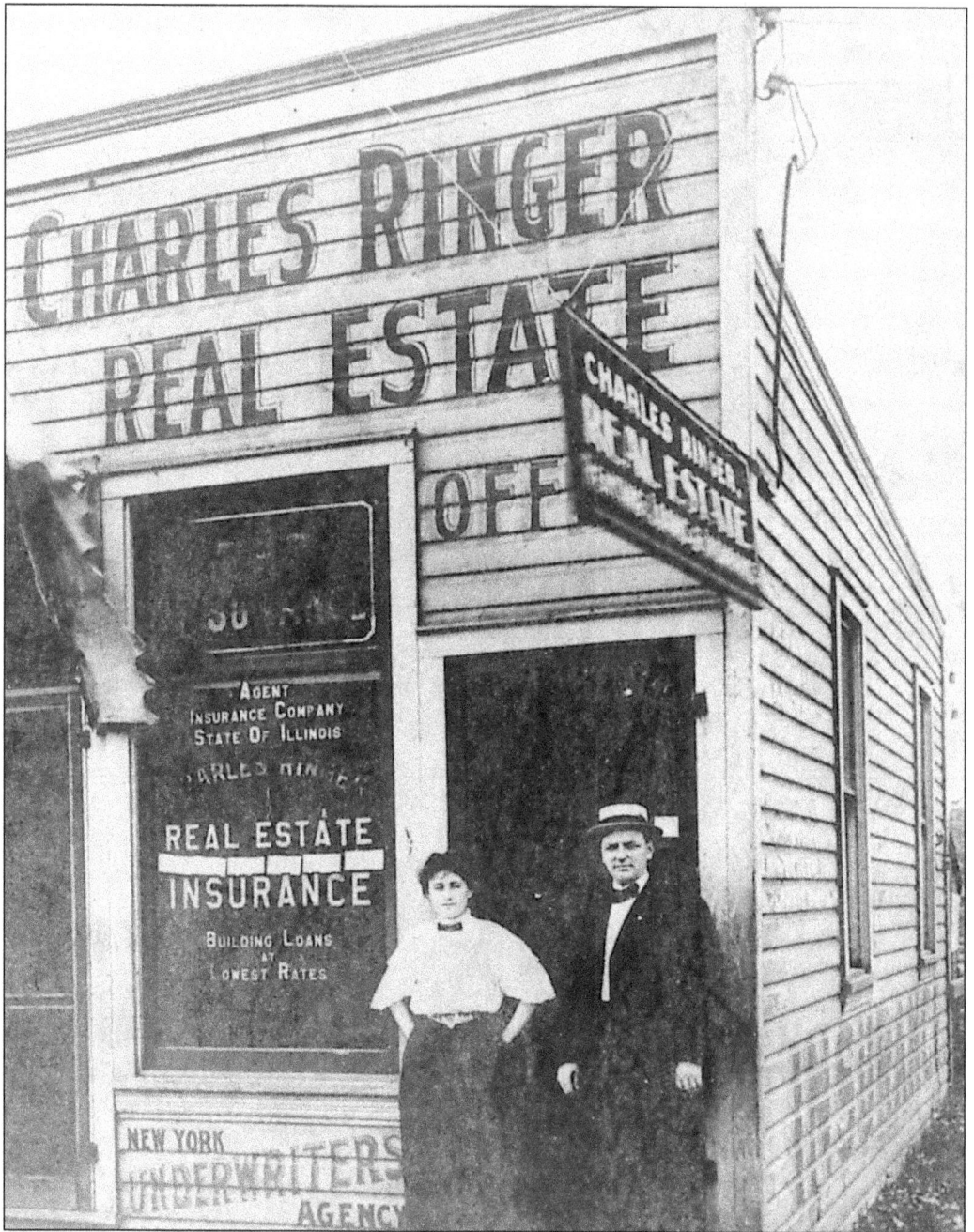

On December 15, 1900, Charles Ringer made his first sale as an independent real estate broker. This first contract, the sale of a property in South Shore to Otto Carlson, was for the grand sum of $1,700, and it would propel Ringer and his family-run business on a trajectory paralleling the success of the community over the next one hundred years. Although he was by no means the only successful businessman trafficking in South Shore land, Ringer's story does have one of the highest profiles. He is seen here in front of his first office at 258 79th Street.

This is another view of 79th Street, this time looking east with Exchange in the foreground.

Ringer Real Estate opened this new office on the site of the original, 79th and Exchange, in 1922.

The interior of Ringer Real Estate is pictured here in the early 1920s. Charles Ringer is in the center of the picture, leaning on the counter. The second person seated to his right is his son-in-law, Morgan Fitch. Fitch would eventually lead the company.

Over the years the company would move several more times, until June 28, 1928, which marked the inauguration of the present home of Ringer Real Estate. The business was designed in a bank-like manner. Cashiers Irene Mihalovitz and Ingrid Carlson are seen waiting on an unidentified customer in this 1928 photograph.

CHARLES RINGER'S
South Shore
SUBDIVISION

WINDSOR PARK GOLF GROUNDS
NEAR LAKE MICHIGAN *AND*
JACKSON PARK

· 🌀 ·

CHARLES RINGER
REAL ESTATE
ESTABLISHED 1900
OFFICES
2480 EAST SEVENTY-FIFTH STREET
COR. KINGSTON AVENUE ❖ SEVENTY-
NINTH STREET & EXCHANGE AVE.

TELEPHONES
SOUTH CHICAGO 110
SOUTH CHICAGO 446

Ringer's purchase of the former Windsor Park Golf Club property in 1918, and his plan to develop it into the South Shore Subdivision, put one of the largest blocks of land in the area up for development. This would also raise Charles Ringer's reputation as a deal maker.

Charles Ringer, seen here in 1900, developed several tracts of land in South Shore, including Tennis Lawn Terrace, the former South Side Tennis Club, and a 20-acre plot called South Shore Addition, at 81st Street and Colfax Avenue. Ironically, his original South Shore Subdivision was never developed as planned. The decision to sell the land to the Armour Institute cut short the development and sale of individual lots to builders.

SPECIAL NEWS BULLETIN

THE ECONOMIST

$5.00 a Year
In Advance in
the United States

£1 5s
in Europe

Single Copies,
10c

OFFICE
108 South LaSalle
Street

Telephone
Franklin · · · · 994

ISSUED EVERY SATURDAY MORNING BY THE ECONOMIST PUBLISHING COMPANY

A WEEKLY FINANCIAL, COMMERCIAL AND REAL ESTATE NEWSPAPER

CHICAGO, WEDNESDAY NOON, FEBRUARY 18, 1920

FOR ARMOUR INSTITUTE

Armour Institute of Technology Purchases From Charles Ringer and Associates 80 Acres, Known as Charles Ringer's South Shore Subdivision, Between 75th and 79th and Yates and Colfax Avenues, for $900,000 and Will Use It for a Permanent Home for This Great Educational Institution.—Profit for the Sellers In Less Than a Year, $422,500.

The Armour Institute of Technology has purchased from Charles Ringer and associates the property formerly occupied by the Windsor Park Golf Club lying between Seventy-fifth street on the north, Seventy-ninth street on the south, Yates avenue on the west and Colfax avenue on the east, comprising 80 acres for $900,000, and will develop at that place a most wonderful educational institution the ultimate investment in the buildings and equipment to be probably $15,000,000. The project has been carried forward and will be developed under the personal supervision of its president, Dr. Frank C. Gunsaulus and J. Ogden Armour, the latter the head of the family and house of Armour & Company.

This is one of the most important developments in an educational way that has taken place not only in this city and state but in this country. Armour Institute was established through the beneficence of the late Philip D. Armour, father of J. Ogden Armour. It will be seen that it is not the intention to permit it to languish but rather the present generation will devote that fine business sense and enterprise which has made them such remarkable leaders in industry and finance to the development of an educational institution, the good of which can never be fully measured.

From a real estate viewpoint the transaction is one of the most notable in the history of the city. It is as important to Chicago as it is surprising. Instead of its development upon the high standard contemplated by Mr.

Ringer and his associates by the sale of vacant land for the construction of apartment houses, dwellings and business blocks, it will of itself bring to that community a population entirely foreign to that which the natural normal development comprehended and it will thus be necessary to extend the boundaries of the city still farther to accommodate the natural normal growth in population and a new development which will follow.

As a piece of real estate enterprise it is as unexpected as anything that could happen. The whole aspect of affairs in that locality has been changed. In THE ECONOMIST of May 31 of last year announcement was made of the purchase of this land by Mr. Ringer and his associates from the Merchants Loan and Trust Company, trustee for the estate of the late John Wentworth, for $477,500. It was the intention of Mr. Ringer and his friends to develop this as a subdivision in the highest style of the art, and it meant a pleasant task for life for Mr. Ringer. Proceeding upon this plan the subdivision was platted, some improvements made, and before they had title to the property a number of lots were sold and the greater part of it could have been disposed of had it been so desired, at a handsome profit, but they went about it slowly because of the fact that they could not get possession until January 1 of this year and furthermore because of the delay and difficulty attending new building construction. Then most unexpectedly this offer to purchase the property came and was accepted.

President Gunsaulus and Mr. Armour, as well as their friends, had looked in many directions with a view to acquiring a site which would meet with their views as to a permanent home for the Institute, but none more desirable could be found.

Mr. Ringer sold under contract probably 57 lots and expended $4,750 for two miles of

sidewalk. The present transaction will net him and his associates a profit of $422,500 for the time which they have held the property. Of the purchase price $100,000 was paid in cash and the remainder is to be paid in monthly installments of $13,333.33 extending over a period of five years with interest at 6 per cent.

This property is interesting because of its history. It comprises 80 acres of vacant land in the center of a thickly developed community, there being many beautiful dwellings, many modest homes, small and large apartment houses and business blocks surrounding it in every direction but so far this land has been untouched, having been under lease and occupied by the Windsor Park Golf Club for many years. It is but a short distance south of the South Shore Country Club. The Windsor Park Station of the Illinois Central is 400 feet away while there are surface car lines in Seventy-fifth and Seventy-ninth streets. The property formerly belonged to the late John Wentworth but his will the income was to go to his daughter Roxanna, now Mrs. Clarence W. Bowen, of New York, and upon her death to her children if living, and if not, to Moses Wentworth if living, and if not, to his children. The matter was taken into the courts by the heirs and Judge Charles M. Walker entered a decree early last year authorizing the sale of the property.

The legal details of the transaction were attended to by Kemper K. Knapp, of Knapp & Campbell.

It will be recalled that Mr. Ringer, the seller, was formerly a member of the board of assessors and when it came to re-election in the fall of 1918 he was counted out. He filed a protest and a recount showed that he was elected by a majority of 4,500 votes and he will be back as County assessor within 30 days.

The future home of the Armour Institute seemed well established in February of 1920; however, due to the untimely death of its president, Dr. Frank C. Gunsaulus, J. Ogden Armour was forced to cancel construction plans, and the property was put back on the market. The Institute later became part of the Illinois Institute of Technology.

SOUTH SHORE PARK

The City of Opportunity

*Eighty Acres—560 Business
and Apartment Lots Ripe
for Immediate Improvement*

75th STREET to 79th STREET
YATES AVE. to COLFAX AVE.

Office on the Premises

75th Street and Yates Avenue

In 1922, after the plans for the Institute fell through, a group of investors purchased the property, and a major development, dubbed South Shore Park, was proposed.

This area, bounded by 79th Street, Yates Avenue, Colfax Avenue, and 75th Street, was previously the site of the Windsor Park Golf Course. After being purchased by former Chicago Mayor (Long) John Wentworth, it was sold by his heirs in 1918 for $500,000 to Charles Ringer. Within three years, this same block of land would change hands twice more, first from Ringer to J. Ogden Armour for $900,000, and then, in July of 1923, to a syndicate of developers.

The South Shore Land Trust, a syndicate of developers, paid $1 million for the property in 1923. They subdivided the land into 560 improved lots, and in turn sold it to smaller, often individual, builders. Within 90 days they reportedly sold $2,746,850 worth of property. In 1924, 32% of the property had been built out and resold at a profit. Forty additional apartment buildings were under construction, providing three hundred additional apartments.

The Ringer Real Estate office, 7915 Exchange, still looks much the same as it did in this 1928 photograph.

A remnant of the Windsor Park Country Club, the Caraval Club—formerly the caddie house at the old golf course—was dismantled on October 10, 1957. It had survived the development of the area in the 1920s.

Four

VIEWS OF THE

NEIGHBORHOOD

The main commercial thoroughfares of South Shore—71st, 75th, and 79th Streets—provided shopping to serve the day-to-day needs of the community. This photograph of 71st and Jeffery was taken in 1954.

The site of the original Bryn Mawr station is again shown here in 1959. Home of the Jeffery Theater and South Shore Bank, this intersection developed into a vital shopping area. Today, as the home of South Shore National Bank, it continues to be an anchor for the neighborhood's economy.

This view from 71st Street and Bennett Avenue looking towards 71st Street and Jeffery Boulevard is from 1968. Compare this with the same view on the bottom of page 14.

This 1968 picture, looking south on Exchange Avenue toward 72nd Street, can be contrasted to the one on the bottom of page 22.

This is a 1959 view looking west on 75th Street from Exchange Avenue, along the northern edge of the South Shore Park development. The northwest corner was the location of the Brown Coal office, pictured on page 16.

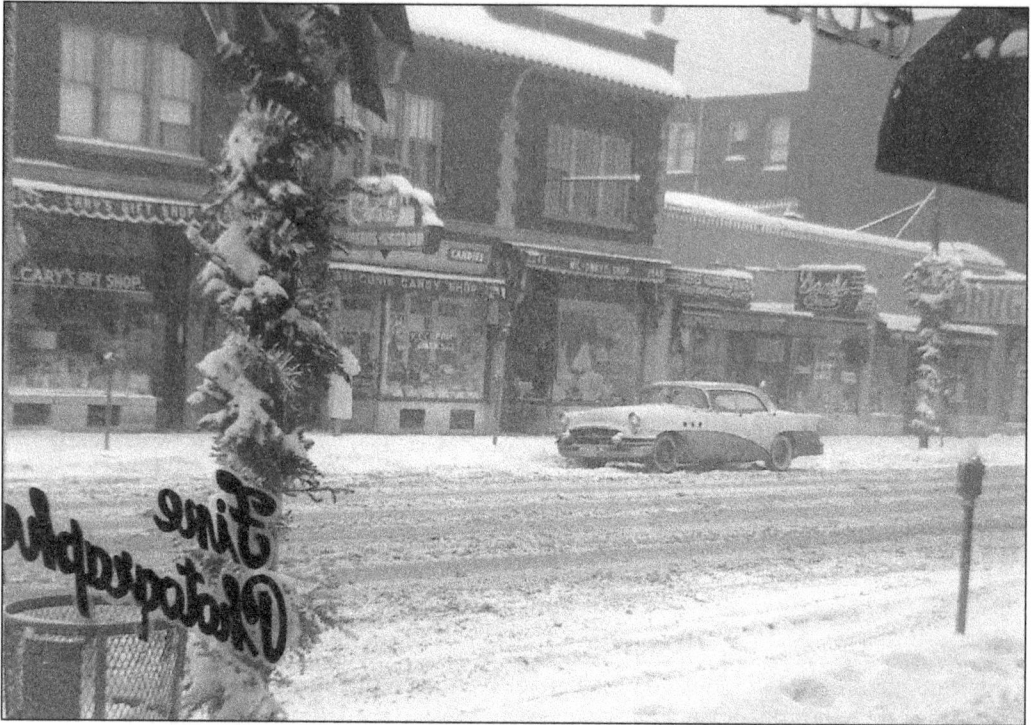

Shown here in 1958, the north side of the 2500 block of 79th Street was the home of Cunis' Candies and Rosenblum's Drugstore.

Another 1958 view shows 79th Street looking east past the Patricia Dress Shop. Rosenblum's Drug Store and Cunis' Candy Shop are on the left. The 1960s would see the Bon Ton Restaurant open on the northwest corner of 79th Street and Colfax Avenue, and a Woolworth built on the southwest corner of the intersection.

Marian Celander greeted customers throughout the 1950s and 1960s at Celander Studio, one of several photography studios servicing the South Shore community. Portraits and weddings comprised the majority of work, along with real estate, legal, and product photography.

Portraits and commercial work were not the only products of Celander Studio. Judy Greitzer was an aspiring dancer when she posed for a 1958 photo shoot.

Samples adorn the walls of the Celander Studio's reception area. The studio closed in 1970.

This building, at 79th Street and Escanaba Avenue, was constructed by George Nord, a relative and associate of Charles Ringer, around 1926. It was one of the first buildings in the Cheltenham area to have a passenger elevator. In addition to the Jewel store, a bowling alley occupied the basement.

This Jewel Food Store at 75th Street and Crandon Avenue was representative of the food chain's "look" in the 1960s. Although some chains existed, most day-to-day needs were met by small, family-owned businesses. Mitchell's Ice Cream shop, Moline's candy store, the Vera Shop, Carl's Hot Dogs, Heiferman's Paints, Clemenson's Flowers, Tews Funeral Home, Rosenblum's Drug Store, Twin Liquors, The Bon Ton Restaurant, and Seder's Clothing store were all examples of independent businesses in the area. Many of the small shops from South Shore subsequently moved to the southern suburbs.

The National Food chain was another icon of the area landscape. This building, which still stands at 115th Place between State and Michigan Avenues, has outlived the chain of grocery stores.

The Crest Sporting Goods store at 79th Street and Euclid Avenue, seen here in a 1960 photograph, rests on the same hunting spot pictured on page 10.

In 1968, Weberg's flower shop stood on the site of the Krause family home at 78th Street and Jeffery Boulevard. The same scene is shown in 1898 on the top of page 11.

Here is another view of Weberg's shop looking north on Jeffery Boulevard to 78th Street. Compare this to the same view from 1895 on the bottom of page 11.

Our Lady of Peace stands at the site of the Krause family farm, also seen at the bottom of page 10.

In 1922, plans to build the South Shore branch of the Chicago Public Library were announced. The English Tudor–style building was to be constructed on city-owned land at 73rd Street and Exchange Avenue and was expected to cost less than $100,000, including the 17,000 books. The building, shown here in 1954, was designed by Paul Gerhardt, the architect responsible for Lane Tech High School and Cook County Hospital.

In September of 1955, construction was underway on the two-story addition to the South Shore YMCA, at 1833 East 71st Street. The "Y" offered recreation facilities, day camp, a pool, and a popular "Hi-Y" program for high school students.

The South Shore Camera Club met at the South Shore YMCA. As part of the Chicago Area Camera Club Association, many members were active in the Chicago Historical Society's Chicagoland in Pictures project, an effort to document the city. Pictured from left to right are: unidentified, Marian Celander, Charlie Genovese, Bill Grady, unidentified, unidentified, unidentified, Joe Barron, unidentified, Bertha Lieberstein, Ray Gedney, and unidentified.

The water filtration plant at 79th Street and Lake Michigan, shown here in 1956, separated Rainbow Beach from the U.S. Steel South Works plant. Before a permanent filtration plant was constructed on the lakefront, an Oglesby Avenue site provided filtered water for those who wanted to bottle their own.

The filtration plant anchors the southern end of Rainbow Beach in this 1954 photograph. The South Works plant of U.S. Steel is in the background.

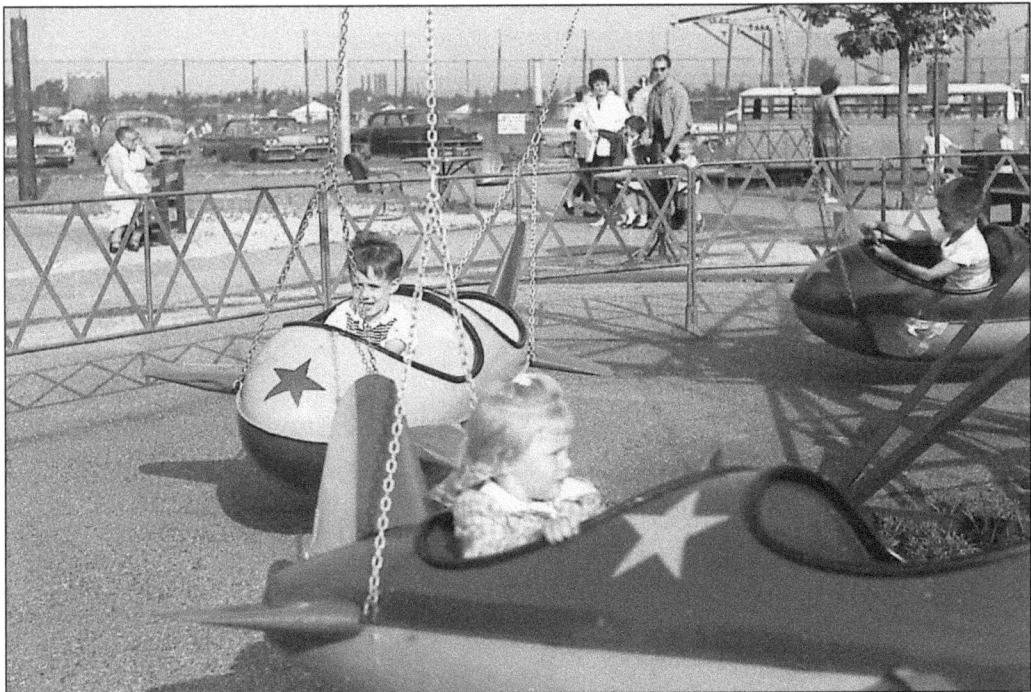

Kiddyland was a landmark on 95th Street in the 1950s and 1960s. Parked next to a go-cart track, the amusement rides attracted families from all over the South Shore area.

The Thunderbird Motel was located at 75th Street and South Shore Drive. The swept roof lines of this local architectural icon echoed the wings of its namesake. An empty lot now perches on this site.

The predominant style of 3-flat apartments, built during the post-World War I housing boom of the 1920s, line Euclid Avenue in this view looking north across 79th Street in 1960.

Looking south on 91st Street at Cregier Avenue, new homes can be seen going up around the Pill Hill area in 1960. The area was nicknamed for the number of doctors living there.

Another view of the Pill Hill area development is shown here, as construction continues just south of 91st Street on East End Avenue.

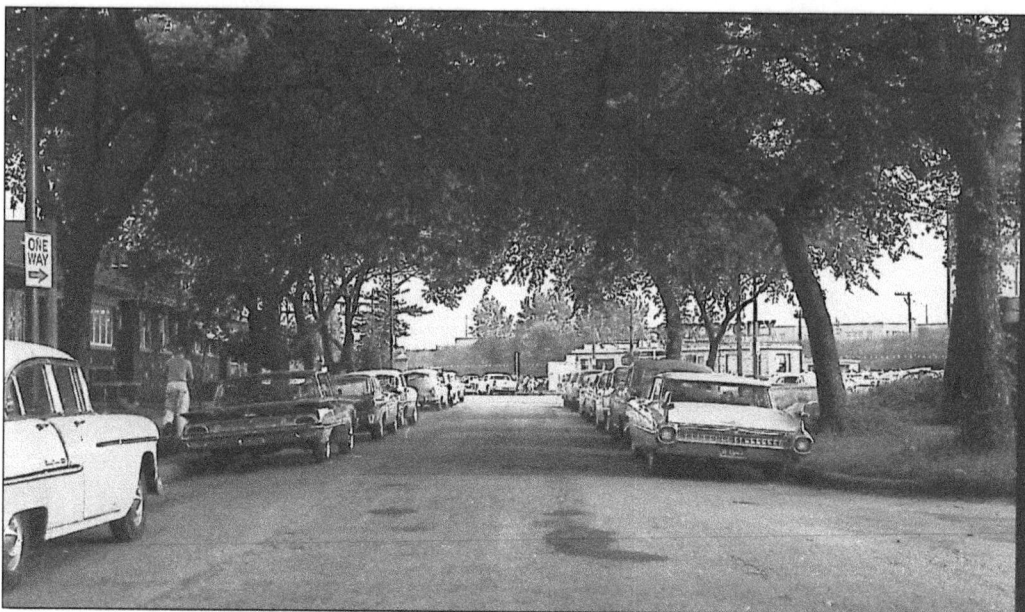

Paxton Avenue, near 84th Street, is beyond the southern border of South Shore (79th Street), but the neighborhoods adjacent to the south represent a transition to the older residential and industrial areas along the Calumet River. This view looks toward 85th Street and South Chicago Avenue.

This high-rise building at 7337 South Shore Drive, shown here in a 1962 photograph, is protected from the lake by a "coffer dam" breakwater. In addition to this unique construction, many of the lots bordering the lake on South Shore Drive were prevented from claiming riparian rights to Lake Michigan itself by the existence of Lake Park Avenue, located slightly off shore, and a narrow lot, also submerged, extending the length of the shoreline. Both appear on early land plats of South Shore developments.

South Shore had its share of celebrities and characters. "Greasy Thumb" Jake Gusik grew up on Maxwell Street and started out as a waiter in a brothel before becoming the financial brains behind Al Capone's gang. He was living in this house on Luella Avenue when he died of a heart attack in 1956 at age 69. Another gangster of note who lived in South Shore was Murray "The Camel" Humphrey, who lived on Bennett Avenue.

Built in 1914, this Prairie Style home located at 2565 East 72nd Place was designed by W.F. Bendir.

This home, located at South Shore Drive and Cheltenham Place, was built as the private residence of South Shore developer Frank X. Ryzetsky.

The few lots that were left undeveloped by the building boom of the 1920s were gradually built upon in the decades after the Depression. These apartments near 67th Street and Chappel Avenue represented a newer style of apartment built in the late 1950s and early 1960s.

Throughout the 1920s and 1930s, the Illinois Central Railroad Suburban Electric lines provided commuter service downtown from South Shore and South Chicago on one branch, from Blue Island on another, and from developing southern suburbs—Homewood, Flossmoor, and Olympia Fields—along the main line. This photograph shows the loop skyline, approaching from the south, in 1938.

The year 1926 brought the first Illinois Central Railroad electric service to the suburban lines. Trains running on electricity, identical to the one pictured here in 1969, replaced the original steam locomotives that had been operating for 70 years.

The 1920s-era station at 76th Street and Exchange Avenue, shown here as it looked in 1969, is another example of the uniform look of the stations after electrification.

The above view along 71st Street looks west toward Stony Island Avenue in 1959.

This scene of a 1957 fire at 2458 East 79th Street was home to Essex Jewelers and Baron's Shoe Store. Tews Funeral Home was located in the next block to the west.

In 1959, the Chicago Fire Department was using a new tool, the snorkel, in fighting fires like this one at the Stewart Lumber Yard at 78th Street and Greenwood Avenue.

The blizzard of 1967 hit South Shore with a vengeance. These bungalows along Oglesby Avenue were buried on January 30, 1967.

This was the view of 79th Street looking east from Yates Avenue.

Everyone took to the streets. Seventy-eighth Street, looking east towards Yates Avenue, was impassable except by foot.

Seventy-ninth Street, between Kingston and Colfax Avenues, was best left to the (sled) dogs. Perhaps it is appropriate that Gordon's Pet Shop is in the background.

On April 21, 1967, the skies darkened over northeastern Illinois and spawned numerous deadly tornadoes. Striking at 4 p.m. on a Friday afternoon, 55 deaths and 400 injuries were reported as a result of the tornadoes. The worst of the twisters stayed on the ground for 16 miles and left a path of destruction across the south side, from Oak Lawn through to South Shore, before moving out over Lake Michigan. The storm downed trees across the Illinois Central Railroad lines at 79th Street and Exchange Avenue.

Looking southwest from 82nd Street and Exchange Avenue, crowds gathered after an F4 tornado tore through the neighborhood, ripping the roof off an apartment building.

Five

THE POLITICAL
PICTURE

Politics in South Shore have largely reflected the traditions of the city. Although dominated by the Democratic Party, a Republican organization was successful in maintaining a strong presence in the neighborhood. Identified in a photograph from election day, June 7, 1909, are, from left to right: Mr. Springer, unidentified, unidentified, Mr. McNamara, Mr. Hoaberg, unidentified I.C. ticket agent, Charles McLaughlin, Andy Gaughn, Augie Wallers, and Gilbert W. Morgan. In addition to a polling place and pool hall, the upper floor of this building was the site of the original Bradwell School in the late 1800s.

"Long" John Wentworth, mayor of Chicago from 1857 to 1858, and again from 1860 to 1861, invested in property throughout the southern region. His purchase of the former Windsor Park Golf Club, and the restrictions on the property after his death, prevented its development until the 1920s.

Mayor Richard J. Daley is seen turning on new streetlights along 73rd Street and Kingston Avenue in 1956. Nicholas J. Bohling, Alderman of the 7th Ward, stands behind the mayor.

Senator Everett Dirksen (R-IL) is shown here with Bill Scannell, Republican Committeeman, at a 1962 rally in South Shore.

Charles Percy, Republican candidate for U.S. Senator, greets a crowd of supporters in South Chicago during his successful 1966 campaign.

Republican candidates pictured here are, from left to right: Paul Wisner, candidate for state senate from the 30th District; Harris Rowe, candidate for state treasurer; and John Stegner, candidate for state representative from the 30th District. They are shown shaking hands for solidarity two weeks before the 1966 elections. Wisner lost to Democrat Dan Daugherty by 60 votes.

Charles Percy (R-IL) speaks on behalf of his party's candidates at the Franko VFW Post on Ewing Avenue in 1966.

State Representative Phillip W. Collins (R-30th District) is shown here in 1966.

The Republican organization in the South Shore area was hard at work putting together a winning campaign in 1966. Pictured outside of their local headquarters are Russell W. Root, 7th Ward committeeman; Don Goff, 8th Ward committeeman; Sheriff Richard Ogilvie, candidate for Cook County board president and later governor of Illinois; and Bill Scannell, State Central committeeman for the 2nd Congressional District.

A former University of Chicago student and an independent Democrat, Abner J. Mikva was elected to Congress from South Shore in 1968, where he served until 1979. He was later appointed as a federal judge.

John Lindsay, mayor of New York City and Republican presidential hopeful, was on the campaign trail in 1968 when he made a stop in South Shore.

Often seen representing the Chicago Teachers Union at political rallies, Tom Reece was an 8th grade science teacher at Myra Bradwell Elementary School when this photograph was taken in 1968. A native of South Shore who had attended Bradwell as a boy, Reece went on to become president of the 40,000-member Chicago Teachers Union and the Illinois Federation of Teachers, both strong forces in Illinois politics.

A social force in the community, the South Shore Commission was started in 1954, with an emphasis on maintaining or improving conditions in the neighborhood. It focused on several areas, including tenant referral, urban renewal, schools, law enforcement, real estate, and human relations. However, the underlying concern of the organization seemed to be the controlled integration and stabilization of the neighborhood.

Rabbi Eric Freidland of Beth Am Temple, at 71st Street and Coles Avenue, is seen in this 1958 photograph with representatives of South Shore Community Church. Pictured from left to right are: Reverend Paul Larson, Reuben Miller, Rabbi Freidland, and Don Upham. Rabbi Freidland was a founding member of the South Shore Commission. It was made up of representatives from civic, political, social, and business groups.

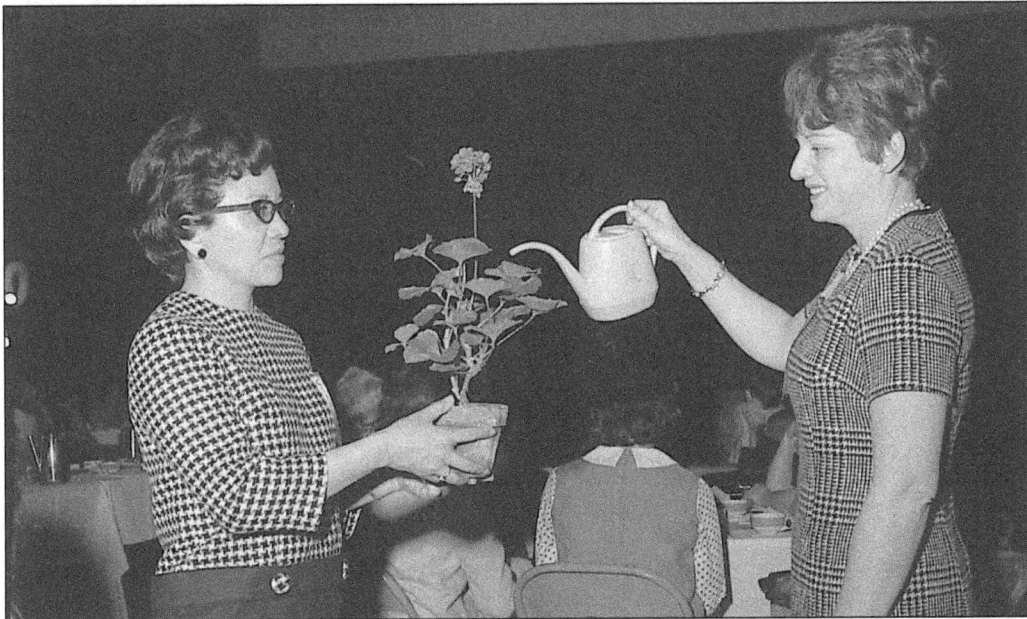

The South Shore Open House Committee, an arm of the South Shore Commission, was formed in the fall of 1963. A public relations force for the community, it hosted an annual open house tour of homes and promoted South Shore as a "stable, interracial, inter-religious community." The symbol for the group, a blooming geranium, is seen here being tended at the group's "Bloomin' Breakfast" event in 1965.

During each open house, volunteer tour guides offered visitors a glimpse of life in South Shore. From bungalow to hi-rise, the event was intended to show off the best of what the community had to offer. Schools, religious institutions, and cultural highlights were featured during the 5th Annual Open House in 1968, which concluded by treating visitors to selections from "Carousel," a production of the Youth Center at 76th Street and Phillips Avenue, that year.

The Open House Committee was made up of over 80 women volunteers, who worked to "sell" South Shore as an ideal place to raise a family.

Six

SCHOOLS, TEMPLES, AND CHURCHES

Up until 1887, South Shore was a community without churches. At that time Reverend George Bird of the South Chicago Congregational Church promoted the need for a religious institution "somewhere between Woodlawn and South Chicago." As a result, a new church was formed. Called by various names—the Duncan Avenue Congregation, the Bethel Congregational, the Windsor Park Congregational, the South Shore Congregational and, finally, the South Shore Community Church—it is seen here in 1956. The South Shore Community Church is located at 74th Street and Yates Avenue.

Myra Bradwell School, eventually named for the ardent feminist and first woman lawyer in Illinois, was established in the 1880s, and was originally called the Duncan Avenue School. It moved from an earlier location on 75th Street, between Exchange and Coles Avenues, to its permanent location at 7710 Burnham Avenue in September of 1889.

Over the years, a sequence of additions extended Myra Bradwell's presence south along Burnham Avenue. The north addition was completed in 1895, and the south addition was added in 1926. The center section was rebuilt in 1937. The north end was used as a satellite for South Shore High School during the 1950s and 1960s. This view looking north on Burnham was taken in 1963 in anticipation of the school's 75th anniversary in 1964.

Pictured above is South Shore Community Church as it stood at 77th Street and Marquette Avenue in 1912. The church was formerly located on the north end of the Bradwell School property, which was sold to the board of education.

The same corner, 77th Street and Marquette Avenue, is seen here in 1968.

This 1958 photograph shows a service in progress at South Shore Community Church. Many of the people who settled or developed South Shore, including the Clemenson, Fitch, and Ringer families, worshipped here.

Reverend Paul Larson was the minister for South Shore Community Church during the late 1950s and early 1960s.

A committee meeting takes place here at South Shore Community Church under the leadership of Reuben Miller.

In 1960, the "All Church Program" at the South Shore Community Church featured skits and performances by members of the congregation.

St. Bride's, the oldest Roman Catholic parish in South Shore, was organized in 1893 by Reverend Timothy D. O'Sullivan of St. Kevin Church at 105th Street and Torrence Avenue. St. Bride's was initially established to serve the 45 or so Catholic families living north of 87th Street in the Cheltenham, Windsor Park, and South Shore neighborhoods.

Land purchased on the east side of Coles Avenue near 78th Street was home to the first church building and, in 1911, became the site for the first Catholic elementary school on the south side. Ground was broken in 1907 for the French Gothic structure that was to be the main building.

Tabor Lutheran Church, at 7950 Escanaba Avenue, served the Swedish community in South Shore beginning in 1900. At that time a Mr. Otto Bergquist led the movement to build the Swedish Evangelical Lutheran Tabor Church, and two lots on the northwest corner of 80th Street and Escanaba Avenue were purchased for $3,000.

Around the turn of the century, a Jewish tailor named Furzinsky reportedly had a shop near 79th Street and Exchange Avenue. It would be more than 20 years later before the community would have its own synagogue. In the early 1920s, Jews from Washington Park began moving in greater numbers to South Shore, and in 1928, the South Shore Temple was founded. Dr. George Fox was the first rabbi, and Louis Kahn headed the congregation of 150. This photograph shows the South Shore Temple at 7215 Jeffery Boulevard in 1954.

Horace Mann School, at 8050 Chappel Avenue, is shown here in 1960.

Reformation Lutheran Church, at 80th Street and Jeffery Boulevard, is seen in this view looking across the Horace Mann schoolyard.

Construction of the foundation for the Akiba Day School, at 6740 South Shore Drive, began in April of 1965. This private school moved to Hyde Park in 1973 and became the Akiba-Schecter Jewish Day School on South Cornell Avenue.

During the 1940s, the increasing German-Jewish population began to meet socially each Sunday morning at the Sinai Temple in Hyde Park. The need arose to establish additional neighborhood congregations, and from these early meetings, two synagogues were eventually built. Congregation B'nai Yehuda, first known as the Hyde Park Liberal Congregation, was established in 1944. Services were first held in rented space, initially in Hyde Park, then in South Shore, until 1960, when the High Holidays were finally celebrated in a permanent site at 82nd Street and Jeffery Boulevard. This photograph of Temple B'nai Yehuda (known as the "Tee-Pee" temple) was taken in November of 1960.

Congregation Habonim, the second congregation born of those early 1940s meetings in Hyde Park, was established at 7550 Phillips Avenue, and it followed Conservative Jewish traditions.

By the 1950s, the Jewish population in South Shore had grown to about 20,000. In addition to Congregation Habonim, another Conservative Jewish synagogue, Congregation B'nai Bezalel, was established and is pictured here in 1960. It was located at 76th Street and Phillips Avenue.

On October 3, 1953, the Hitterman wedding party posed in front of Our Lady Gate of Heaven, at 2338 East 99th Street, for a group portrait. Celander Studio would document another Hitterman family wedding and photograph many of the Hitterman children over the next decade.

South Shore High School, at 7626 Constance Avenue, is shown here in 1954. The high school opened its doors in 1940. Marie Von Brewster was the school's first principal.

The view above, taken in 1955, shows 75th Street and Euclid Avenue, looking south towards South Shore High School.

Construction of St. Phillip Neri Catholic Church, at 2132 East 72nd Street, was begun in 1926 and completed in 1928, with the first mass celebrated on Easter Sunday of that year. Designed by Joseph W. McCarthy, whose other South Shore works included Our Lady of Peace, this building reflected a combination of Gothic influences. When first built, it was termed "South Shore Gothic-1928." It is constructed of Plymouth Granite and Bedford Stone, with a copper and tin spire that rises 164 feet above the church.

Andrew Rebori designed the Gothic Revival architecture of Bryn Mawr Community Church, at 7000 South Jeffery Boulevard, in 1916.

94

St. Margaret's Episcopal Church, at 2555 East 73rd Street, is shown as it appeared in 1959.

The Reverend H. William Barks Jr., along with unidentified members of St. Margaret's Episcopal Church, watch as their Episcopal bishop performs a 1955 groundbreaking ceremony.

The South Shore Baptist Church, located at 3053 East Cheltenham Place, was officiated by Reverend Donald E. Anderson, an active member of the South Shore Ministerial Association. The group, made up of clergy from various denominations, was active in trying to stabilize the community during the 1960s.

Thomas Hoyne Public School was located at 89th Street and Crandon Avenue.

The Greek Orthodox St. Constantine & Helen Church, located at 73rd and Stony Island Avenue, was still under construction in February of 1953, when this photograph was taken. Reverend Mark E. Petrakis had moved the congregation from a former location at 61st Street and Michigan Avenue.

The noted Chicago author Harry Mark Petrakis, son of the Reverend Petrakis, also lived in South Shore. This photograph from 1958 was used on the dust jacket of his first book, *Lion at My Heart*.

St. Constantine & Helen School was located directly behind the church on Stony Island Avenue. It was one of only three Greek Orthodox Schools in Chicago.

The First Presbyterian Church, at 6400 South Kimbark Avenue, was one of the earliest area churches. Organized in May of 1860, its original members included Paul Cornell, the founder of Hyde Park, who donated the first church building, a small white chapel on Hyde Park Avenue.

The sanctuary of the First Presbyterian Church of Hyde Park is seen here during a 1958 choral concert. The church served members of the Woodlawn, Hyde Park, and Jackson Park Highland neighborhoods.

A church banquet held the same year is pictured here at the First Presbyterian Church of Hyde Park.

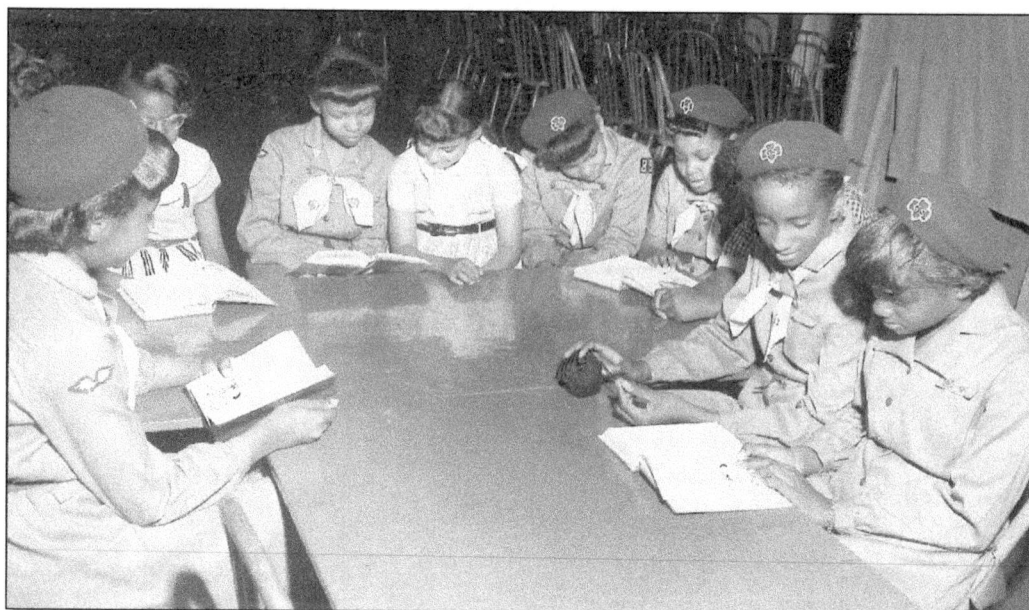

These Girl Scout and Boy Scout troops, meeting at the First Presbyterian Church, reflect the racial makeup of the Woodlawn neighborhood in the late 1950s. After World War II, the population of Chicago's African-American community expanded and, with housing in short supply, many black families began moving to South Shore, following in the footsteps of the working-class Irish and German families before them.

The First Presbyterian Church promoted an image of integration and unity in the late 1950s.

The 18th Church of Christ Scientist, designed by Charles Faulkner, was located at 7262 Coles Avenue.

Our Lady of Peace Catholic Church, at 2000 East 79th Street, was organized in 1919 to serve the 78 catholic families living in the area at that time. The grammar school associated with the church opened in 1923, with the completion of a new school building delayed by the Depression until 1933. This Italian Renaissance–style church was designed by Joseph W. McCarthy. In the late 1940s and early 1950s, children attending OLP could enjoy 5¢ donuts and 15¢ hamburgers across the street at Moline's candy store.

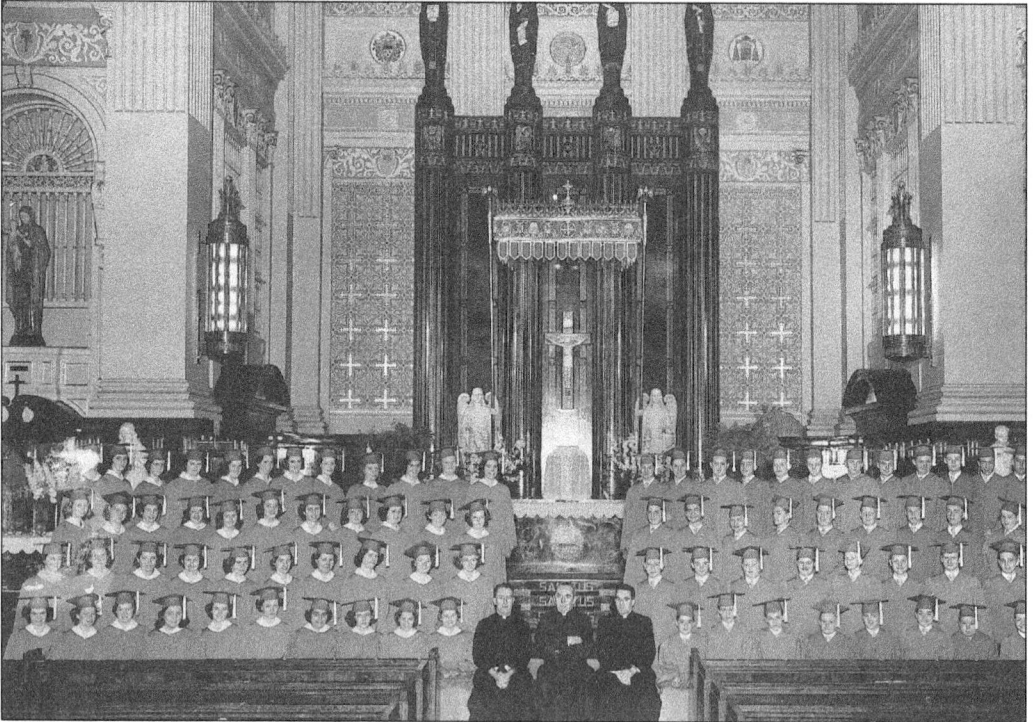

A graduating class from Our Lady of Peace Catholic School poses in the sanctuary in 1948.

In addition to St. John's Methodist Church, at 7350 South Jeffery, two other Methodist congregations—Southfield Methodist at 1750 East 78th Street, and South Shore Methodist at 7851 Burnham Avenue—served South Shore in 1961.

Bethany Lutheran Church, at 92nd Street and Jeffery Avenue, is shown here in 1956.

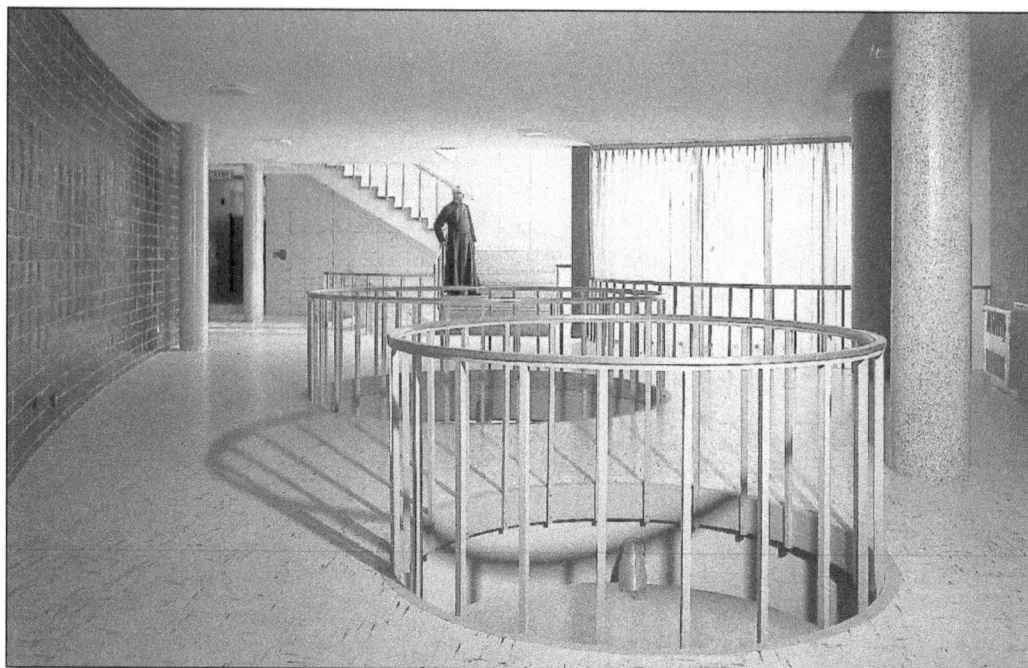

In 1888, St. Francis De Sales began serving the community, at 102nd and Avenue J. It was started as a mission of the largely German St. Peter and Paul parish in South Chicago. In 1910 the cornerstone was laid for a combination church and school near 101st Street and Ewing Avenue and, in 1925, after near destruction by fire, the high school program was expanded, with continued expansion into the 1930s. This photograph, taken in 1958, celebrates a modern addition to the school.

The library of St. Francis de Sales High School is seen here in 1958.

Reverend Alfred C. Crouch was minister of the South Shore Presbyterian Church, located at 2824 East 76th Street, around the time this photograph was taken in 1960.

Zion Lutheran Church, at 85th Street and Stony Island Avenue, is shown here in 1956. The church continues its traditions at the same site today.

St. George's Catholic Church was organized in 1903 by Reverend John Kranjec. Originally located on 95th Street, between Avenues M and N, the parish served the immigrant populations surrounding the steel mills. The Gothic-style building pictured here is located at 96th Street and Ewing Avenue.

The South Chicago Community Center, located at 9135 South Brandon Avenue, was formerly known as the Bird Memorial Church. It is seen here in 1960.

Seven

VIEW FROM THE SKYWAY

The Chicago Skyway cuts across the south side of Chicago, skirting the edge of South Shore as it follows along the path of South Chicago Avenue. It connects with the Dan Ryan Expressway at its northernmost point, and with Interstate 80 and the Indiana Tollway at its southernmost point. In so doing, the Skyway provides a direct route to both the industrialized areas of northwest Indiana and the vacation territory of southwestern Michigan.

Built in the late 1950s, the construction progress was photographed regularly. One week before opening, the photographer was allowed to roam at will along the empty highway.

This is a 1954 view looking north on Stony Island Avenue towards 79th Street, with the Mall Tool building on the left. Four years later the Chicago Skyway would carve a thruway to Northwest Indiana and Michigan, passing over this intersection.

In October of 1957, the first span linking the Chicago Skyway across 79th Street was laid into place. The location, at the convergence of 79th Street, Stony Island, and South Chicago Avenues, was also the home of the Grand Crossing Tack Company (the building beyond the Skyway). E.W. and O.N. Hutchinson started the company in 1883.

Shown here is the entrance to the Skyway from 79th Street.

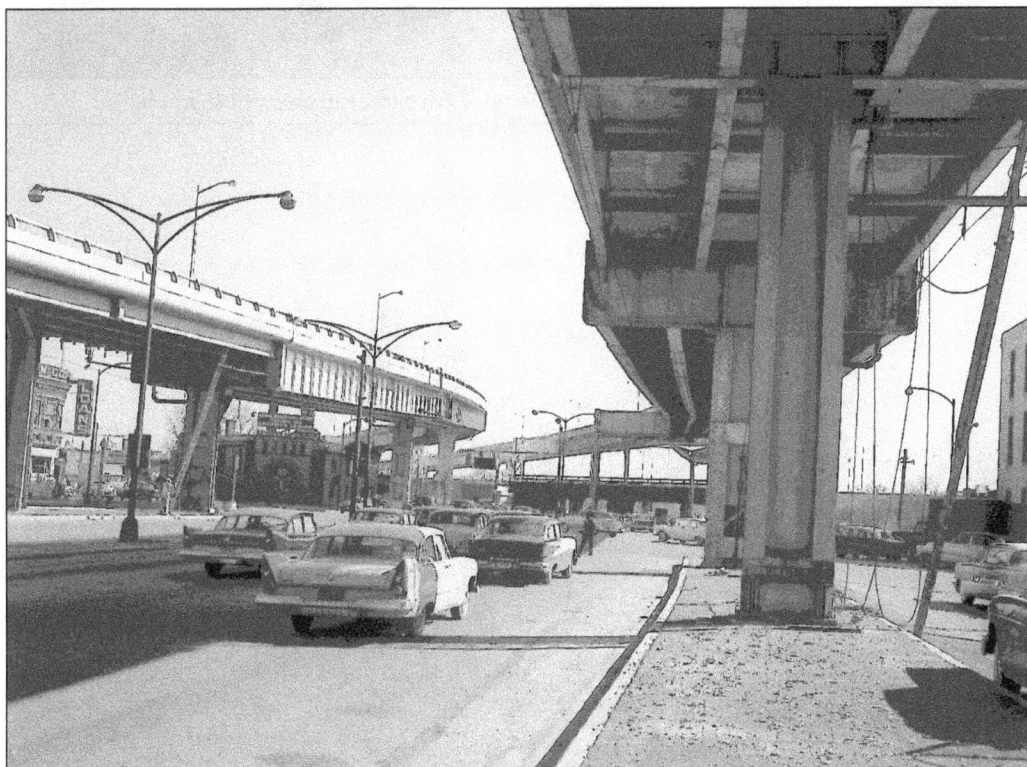

In 1922, the *Chicago Daily News* reported that the intersection of 79th Street and Stony Island Avenue, near Grand Crossing, was "destined to be South Shore's busiest spot . . . past which flows a large traffic." Although the writer was correct, he could not have foreseen that the greatest amount of traffic would glide by, high above the streets, soon after this 1957 picture.

Construction is nearly complete on a section above 79th Street in this photograph.

This view is north from the tollway exit ramp onto Stony Island Avenue, above 79th Street and South Chicago Avenue.

A tollway oasis is nearing completion in 1957.

The construction of the bridge over the Calumet River began in early 1957. Construction workers made $3-3.50 per hour building the toll road.

This view is from the Skyway, looking over the Calumet River toward the bridge at 100th Boulevard.

From the Skyway bridge, a coal barge on the Calumet River can be seen leaving the Commonwealth Edison station at 100th Boulevard. The Cal Sag Channel system, connecting to the Little Calumet River, brought coal up from Southern Illinois through Indiana.

This is the view looking northeast from the Skyway bridge toward the train bridge across the Calumet River.

Looking east toward the bridge over the Calumet River, this photograph was taken one week before the tollway was officially opened in 1958.

An individual account by O.M. Hutchinson describes the South Chicago steel mill area as he found it in 1881. Among the sand dunes he describes a huge hole being dug, which was to be the first blast furnace of the new Bessemer Steel Plant being constructed by the North Chicago Rolling Mills Company. The company would soon change its name to Illinois Steel and, eventually, U.S. Steel would locate its huge South Works here. As the dunes were leveled, the lake was also filled in with cinders, slag, and ashes. Over the years the mills crept out across the landfill onto the lake, until reformers put a stop to lakefront development. This pushed industry farther south along Lake Michigan and helped establish Gary, Indiana, as a steel town.

This 1954 aerial view peers down into the workings of U.S. Steel's South Works Plant, which extended south from 79th Street and the lake to the Calumet River. The slag from the area's early steel mills was used to fill in the streets of the south side, raising them above the water level of the surrounding sloughs.

114

In the mid-1800s a debate began—the backers of the Chicago River versus those of the Calumet River—for dominance in developing the region. On one side were eastern railroad interests, who saw the Calumet area as a logical choice for rail and water terminals, and on the other side were real estate interests, whose investments were focused around the Chicago River.

Not least among the Chicago backers was the soon-to-be-mayor "Long" John Wentworth. Needless to say, the Chicago property owners got their way, and the Calumet region took a back seat to real estate development to the north.

In the 1880s, South Chicago and Irondale were rife with steel mills. The product of the blast furnaces gave Irondale its name and, over the decades, gave families the opportunity to spend summer nights watching men dump molten slag along Torrence Avenue, a tradition as spectacular as fireworks on the Fourth of July.

In 1959, the glow of U.S. Steel's South Works lit up the night sky, reflecting off the Calumet River.

Eight

VIEWS OF THE CITY

The building of quality, single-family homes and three-flat apartments, combined with the ease of transportation, gave South Shore the air of a bedroom community. Many of the residents commuted south to the steel mills or north to the Loop. Commuters going north or south retraced the history of the area each time they traveled the Illinois Central Electric line. What follows are a few highlights.

Robie house, at 5757 West Woodlawn, remains a highlight of Hyde Park's architectural heritage. Designed by Frank Lloyd Wright in 1906, it is one of his last prairie-style houses. The house is shown here in a photograph from 1959.

Located in West Pullman, not many realize that another Frank Lloyd Wright design graces the south side. The Stephen A. Foster house and stable, built in 1900, is said to represent a rare variation on a Japanese architectural style for Wright. The debut of the Japanese Ho-o-den pavilions at the 1893 World's Fair, which put Japanese architecture on display in America for the first time, may have been an influence on Wright's design for this West Pullman residence.

The Southmoor Hotel was built on Stony Island Avenue overlooking Jackson Park in 1924. The grand building was later turned into apartments, before eventually being torn down.

The Southmoor Hotel (right), at the intersection of 67th Street and Stony Island Avenue, is shown here in 1954.

This view is looking south on Stony Island Avenue toward the Jackson Park Hotel. The Southmoor can be seen on the right.

The Edward A. Turner house, located at 4935 South Greenwood in Hyde Park, was built in 1888 and was designed by Solon S. Beman. The young architect from New York had moved to Chicago in 1879 to design Pullman, the nation's first planned company town. He also designed the Washington Park Club and several of the buildings at the World's Columbian Exposition of 1893.

The year 1958 brought urban renewal to Hyde Park. I.M. Pei and Lowenberg designed the University Apartments, at 1451 East 55th Street, seen here in a 1962 photograph. Built in 1961, they were a product of the Hyde Park Redevelopment Project, constructed in an effort to stem the flight of the middle class from the neighborhood.

Also part of the Hyde Park Redevelopment Project, townhouses, like the ones shown here in a 1962 photograph taken along Kenwood Avenue, replaced dilapidated structures cleared through urban renewal. The modern style of townhouses introduced in the area were variously designed by I.M. Pei and Harry Weese & Associates and are credited for the resurgence of the townhouse in a modern setting.

In the 1950s the Harding Museum, at 4853 Lake Park Avenue, displayed an eclectic array of armor, antiques, and art in a castle-like setting. The collection was the obsession of the late George F. Harding.

Suits of armor, displayed on life-sized mannequins, were posed among the collections of swords, crossbows, and curiosities. The collection is also reported to have included a bed used by Napoleon on his Egyptian campaign, and pianos that belonged to Liszt and Chopin.

Harding, a real estate operator, aviation enthusiast, and political leader, amassed the bulk of the collection, begun by his father, George F. Harding Sr., in the late 1800s. The Harding Museum was housed in an addition built onto the collector's Victorian home and was made public after his death.

Artifacts were collected by Harding from all over the world and flown back to the museum by private jet.

Fourteen hundred pieces of the Harding Collection now reside at the Art Institute of Chicago, making the Art & Armament collection at the Institute the third largest in the U.S. More than two hundred of the artifacts are on public display.

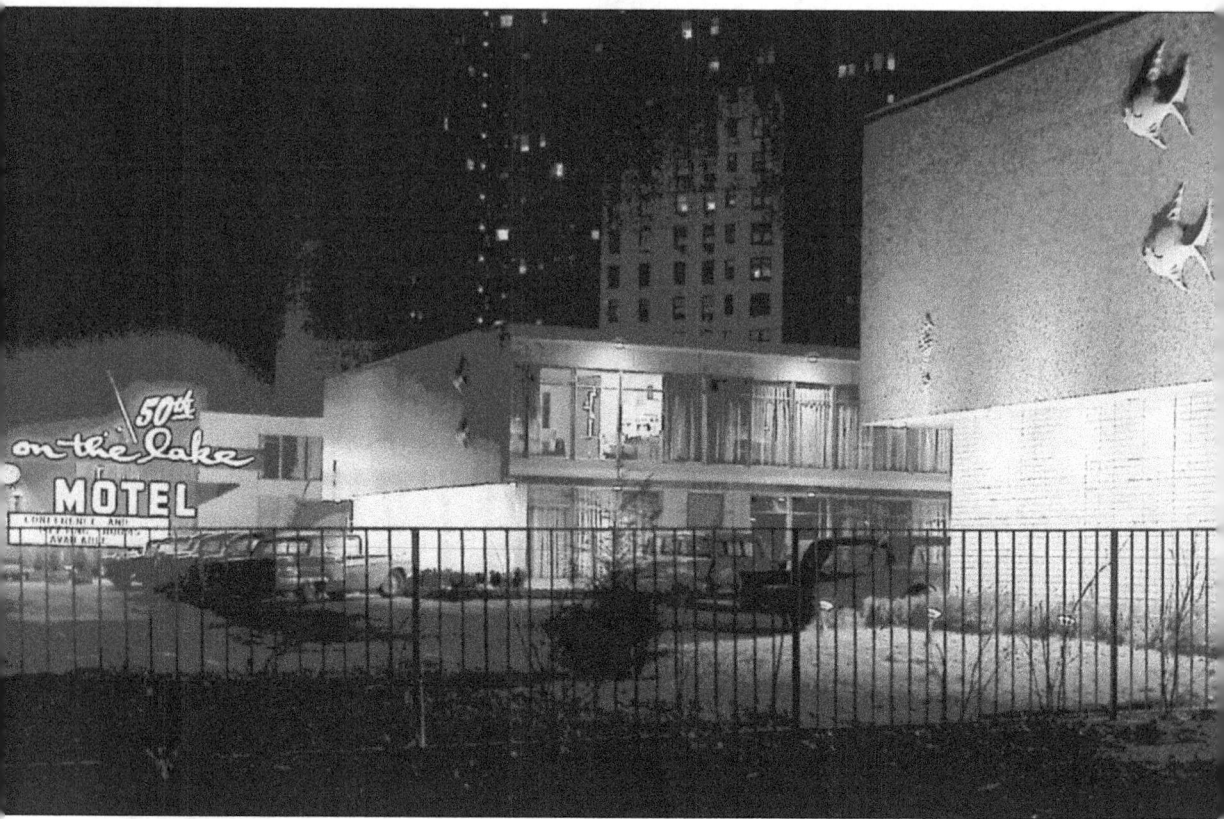

This 1959 night view shows the 50th on The Lake Motel, a Lake Shore Drive landmark in the 1950s and 1960s.

This is the skyline as it appeared from the south side in the 1960s.

The sun sets over the Chicago skyline in the 1950s.

ACKNOWLEDGMENTS

This book would not have been possible without the assistance and support of the following people:

My father, Hugh Celander, provided both the initial collection of photographs and the inspiration for this book. My mother, Marian Celander, provided a lifetime of encouragement for all of my projects. Without the support of my wife, Melani Davis (raised in Jeffery Manor), this book would not have been possible. Big hugs go to my daughters, Jenny and Anna Celander, who had to do without a full-time father during much of the summer this book was completed.

Special thanks to: Charles Fitch of Ringer Real Estate and Bob Zemhme of Clemenson's Florist, who supplied historical information and photographs from their personal collections. Thanks also to all those who contributed both directly and indirectly to this volume including: Dominic Pacyga, Paul Johnson, Joyce Fulgium and Carol Bryant of Columbia College Chicago, Tom Grant of The Illinois Central Railroad Historical Society, June Neet at the Art Institute of Chicago, Bob Celander, Harris Davis, John Ostenburg, Bob Nixon, Mary Ann Rosenblum, Edith and Walter Strauss, Bert Heiferman, Rabbi LeoWolkow, Henry and Trudi Altman, Dorothy Hitterman, Burt Springer, Judy Greitz, Don Goff, and many others who helped identify events, buildings, and people. Thanks also go to Michael Rabiger; Emily Reible; Chap Freeman; Judd Chesler; Chris Swider; Ric Coken; Eileen Dominick; Usama Alshaibi; Sandy Cuprisin in the Film and Video Department of Columbia College; and Mike Weiss, Colleen Newquist, and Tom Teshima for their support and encouragement, and for listening to me rant about photography and South Shore. Finally, a heartfelt thank you to Miss O'Keeffe of Myra Bradwell, who gave me an E+ on a much more condensed version of this book back in 1968.

For updated information on Chicago's South Shore, visit our website:
www.chicagosouthshore.com.

www.ingramcontent.com/pod-product-compliance
Lightning Source LLC
Chambersburg PA
CBHW080853100426
42812CB00007B/2015